The National Poetry Series was established in 1978 to ensure the publication of five collections of poetry annually through five participating publishers. The Series is funded annually by Amazon Literary Partnership, William Geoffrey Beattie, the Gettinger Family Foundation, Bruce Gibney, HarperCollins Publishers, The Stephen and Tabitha King Foundation, Padma Lakshmi, Lannan Foundation, Newman's Own Foundation, Anna and Olafur Olafsson, Penguin Random House, the Poetry Foundation, Amy Tan and Louis DeMattei, Amor Towles, Elise and Steven Trulaske, and the National Poetry Series Board of Directors.

THE NATIONAL POETRY SERIES WINNERS
OF 2020 OPEN COMPETITION

Borderline Fortune by Teresa K. Miller
Chosen by Carol Muske-Dukes for Penguin Books

Requeening by Amanda Moore
Chosen by Ocean Vuong for Ecco

[*WHITE*] by Trevor Ketner
Chosen by Forrest Gander for the University of Georgia Press

Philomath by Devon Walker-Figueroa
Chosen by Sally Keith for Milkweed Editions

Dear Specimen by W. J. Herbert
Chosen by Kwame Dawes for Beacon Press

[WHITE]

[WHITE]

POEMS

by Trevor Ketner

SELECTED BY
FORREST GANDER

The University of
Georgia Press
Athens

Published by the University of Georgia Press
Athens, Georgia 30602
www.ugapress.org

Designed by Kaelin Chappell Broaddus
Set in 10.5/13.5 Garamond Premier Pro Regular
by Kaelin Chappell Broaddus

Most University of Georgia Press titles are
available from popular e-book vendors.

Printed digitally

Library of Congress Control Number: 2021937800
ISBN: 9780820360393 (pbk.: alk. paper)
ISBN: 9780820360409 (ebook)

for Cormac
who walks with love
so slowly through museums

I simply want to present people with their ruins.

—ROBERT RAUSCHENBERG (1987)

Score for [*White*]

[WHITE]

Each time I enter the retrospective:
quickness, sanguine intensity

                    and for a moment I have
to stop, everyone milling around

me and the art in the middle. Then I lock
in again, a secret

compartment in the heel of a spy's shoe

once the smuggled thing
—a square

                    of mud or gold or
                    toilet paper, white lead

paint (so heavy)—
has been removed.

[

Rauschenberg instructs someone to write
on the back of *Erased de Kooning
Drawing*, "DO NOT REMOVE
DRAWING FROM FRAME / FRAME
IS PART OF DRAWING," which is just that,
a drawing that's been erased—an undrawing.

[

After he, Rauschenberg,
reclaims paper's beforeness,
it sits on the wall—
a scrim bustle scrape smudge
of sound applied behind it
as to a stage being set.

[

A letter from Robert Rauschenberg to the cast of *Open Score* (1966):

This is identification and instructions.

The stage director will direct you to move quietly upstairs and wait for your entrance. You will enter into the darkness and wait for cues. This is a continuous piece and your entrance should be made as quietly and smoothly as possible.

[

Open Score was a large-scale performance piece staged at the Armory as part of a nine-night performance series. The center of the piece was an unchoreographed tennis match between two players. Each tennis racket was wired to sound whenever it made contact with the ball; they sounded like bells in a bell tower—each chime shut off a light until the arena went totally dark. Once darkness was complete, a group of some five hundred people entered, announced their names, and faced the audience. Their ghost images were caught with infrared cameras (cutting edge technology at the time) and projected onto large screens around the arena: miniature/magnified mirror of the crowd/each ghost respectively, a shadow mimicry.

[

LARGE NUMBERS WILL BE YOUR DIRECTOR. *The activities that must be executed are listed below and should be memorized. These will not necessarily appear in the order listed.*

o – The Fool .

Wearing that dress (the floral print)
        with goldenrod tights,

I say *of course* and mean *I'm queer as fuck.*
There are no cliffs in Minneapolis
        because there are no mountains.

Sky is not normally yellow—and yet.
Here are my thick boots. I forget

to shave my beard, so it grows wild, thicket-thick.
I say *of course* and mean *o is in the middle of the number*
        line between every possible positive

and negative. White flower in hand is flat—
        flowers stitched thin into dress are flat.

I grew my hair last winter, bleached it.
        I feel as if I'm supposed to feel
like I want something—I've already got

emerald slippers people on the street say they love.
I've got a stick I carry with me.

The stars are up there, behind that color.
I look for them, fall down the non-mountain,
        down the horizontal cliff—no one tells you
there's a trail down there, but there is.

When asked, de Kooning provided a drawing
he thought would be
especially difficult to erase completely—
charcoal and crayon, pencil, oil, and ink.

Pulling it from the easel, de Kooning said,
"I want it to be something I'll miss."

[

I—TOUCH SOMEONE WHO IS NOT TOUCHING YOU.

I – The Magician .

Line, warped, above his head:
        white headband. Under red
table: white lilies, pink anemones.

On table: an espresso, butter knife,
        overpriced chocolate croissant,
        stirring stick (recyclable). In his hand

a box of straws to fill the jar by the window.
        On cold days he wears a red sweater.
I found out he has two kids—

he seems as young as anyone,
an atmospheric man.
                I just continue failing

to see myself in the water glass again,
        flowers from my dress, beard, nothing
twisting in pulses across the surface.

I'll get up, pour more water in the glass,
ask him to conjure another curve
        of white, more of the red in it. He points

outside. Another accident:
tan sedan tail bitten by
identical sedan—hubcap, star.

Bed (1955)

oil, pencil, toothpaste
and red fingernail
            polish on pillow,
quilt, and bedsheet
mounted on wooden supports

[

Looking into the undrawing again,
I can see it—can you?—the gap
left in a body after a bone breaks,

            just a small bone, a toe maybe,
something that'll heal right up
quite naturally,

that would have, ultimately, been forgotten.

[

A bone on the stage of a box no bigger
than a tube of lipstick
            becomes a miniature monument.

[

All art is violence, a positive strain,
damage intent on

            rebuilding—the precision
of an urban construction company,

taking to mud a pocket
of steel-shape and glass-shape.

Mud, like a square of old newspaper,
like paint, suggests

what we have can be more _____
once we've torn it down.

[

Rauschenberg, *thinking of doing a self-portrait of inner man*, prints X-rays of his forty-two-year-old body with a planetary chart for 1967, the year it (his forty-two-year-old-body and the piece) is completed, printed over the X-ray in red ink. It is, at the time, the largest hand-pulled print in the world.

[

You tell me that is very gay
and I smile because you are right
and we are also very gay,
gay enough to think it's a good idea.

[

I started using real objects from the very first.
I remember in the navy I painted a picture of someone
and I didn't know much about painting,
I used blood for the red—my blood.

[

He was a Libra;
of course he was.

2 – The High Priestess .

While single I knew a woman.

We talked while waiting for the bus.
Often cold, as winter will be
in Minnesota, we bundled—blue scarf
around her neck, cap with a moon stitched in.

She carried a book, even when it snowed

at night on her return, the actual hung moon
like a blackened nail on a crushed toe.
She told me about having to shave
to keep her five o'clock shadow from coming in.

She told me the doctors had done blood work—

she would start estrogen injections.
Sitting on the cold, metal line of that bench,
for the first time that winter I felt
happy for someone, felt how much potential

the world has for joy—it dwells in us

like a light left on accidentally coming
home from a night out. I thought of her
last week, as we started packing—I pulled
the sheet from the window—too poor

for drapes—pomegranates, slender palms.

I wanted to write this whole thing by hand,
scrawl it out like a signature. I wanted the words

like a forgery, to come out
layer upon layer upon lay-

er over a ground invisible,
so thick is their language.

[

[ERASED JOHN ASHBERY POEM]

[

I wonder if Rauschenberg, hunched
over de Kooning's drawing, felt
as I did typing that Ashbery poem
and erasing it,
that he was hollowing himself out—

if he thought as I just have:

There is so much here
I want to leave
for you.

[

Forty erasers to get back to paper,
says Rauschenberg, if you believe him.

One tap and the Ashbery poem
is gone, though in the world
already, it can be found again.

Can this be what we mean by *resilience*?

3 – The Empress .

She bought three copper watering cans
for her terrariums, in which she tended fragile

succulents on the nightstand next to her bed.
Once a mouse nuzzled into the soil.

The couch, flower-red, shifted its cushions.
Her roommate bought the couch before they moved in

having met only once when they visited
the city we all live in now—for now.

Her hair has grown so much since then—wild
crown—like the one she keeps on the plush skull

by the door, her scarves hung there like water.
We are sitting in the middle of so much

bread—a state of it, two, three. From here
it's beyond everything: the horizon, the river

breaking from the sea behind the priestess
in her moon cap into the city. But the succulent

crown grows like roots in fields, histories beneath,
constant pull forward, silent unreadiness
            to be buried, to dig, archaeology

of the bonds of women, of heavy witching hours—
at night, she tells me, she can't sleep.

4 – The Emperor .

I'm afraid to return to the desert,
where, yes, you'll find flowers, but not on my dress;
I don't wear my dresses in the desert—only armor,
a red blanket. My desert hair is always brown.

The high desert has many mountains and so
many cliffs. I won't walk off them—a small apple,
unripe, rolls off a granite countertop—
I'm watched in the desert. Rams' heads

grow along the tips of dead ground cover. As a child
I pulled them, like nails, from my hands;
then itch under skin, unscratchable, then red,
a bloodletting in natural pearls. In the mountains,

the copper river dwindles to a thread.
The mountain is dead from a fire five years ago,
undergrowth, if it's there anymore, char-cloaked.
My high school nearly burned down, too—yellow

cinder block, racist murals, and all. Still
a small wooden house in the woods nestled over
the desert, the mountain an orange smear before nightfall.

He's got the gold world in his hand—
when you come from the desert its laws never leave you.

Rauschenberg asks the Swedish museum
            housing some of his *White*
Paintings to repaint them.

In the note, he doesn't care
who repaints them,
so long as they are repainted

            with a roller using house paint,
like a wall in someone's studio apartment.

He says, *I didn't want their past*
            to be a mark on them. . . .
They have no history.

[

            To hide the mars and marks
            of each piece of white preserves

the violent history of white
in the new white it shapes from beneath.

[

"Untitled," still a name, is a history.

5 – Hierophant .

On the Washington Ave Bridge one can stand
on the spot Berryman once did, seeming to think
there were four worlds—bridge, air,
river, moon against river—that by passing
through he'd find the keys to the kingdom

of being okay, and maybe, at the bottom he did.
He dreamt in a strange tongue—old music.
There are poets living now who've tried
to sing his songs—but he knew
secrets early: the father has been gone

a long while, name so plain it's unforgettable—
there's nothing extraordinary about grief but that it is
inexhaustible, impossible to drown even
in the green waters of the resurrected dead—
intoxication, blur. It was the west

bank, where they found him. Had he missed
completely the river? In the end,
there are only so many prayers,

and the rest is butter on toast—a great strip of holy
symbology down the front of a shirt, a quiet
gesture in the photograph, an expressive hand.

Rauschenberg began painting *White Lead Painting*

in a Fulton Street studio before moving to another studio on Front Street in 1955. The piece had amassed so much paint and material, it was too large and heavy to move. Rauschenberg left it, only taking one small square.

[

Charles Olson and Rauschenberg are both at Black Mountain College where Olson is said to have often used the following poem to teach; Rauschenberg, at some point, must hear it:

> whatever you have to say, leave
> the roots on, let them
> dangle
>
> And the dirt
>
> Just to make clear
> where they come from

[

I would fuck Rauschenberg in his studio
to make it, like a pastoral necktie,

into a combine. I'd plan it so it would be 1955.

I made the museum
attendants nervous

when I leaned in
to look at *Bed*, not sure myself

that I wouldn't crawl into it
and dream a dream drawn-on like the pillow
in Twombly's shake scribble shimmer scrawl.

[

The day after writing that, I return to MoMA
and read the following quote from Rauschenberg
on the museum didactic for *Bed*:

One of the friendliest pictures I've ever painted.
My fear has always been that someone would want to crawl into it.

[

Fear that someone would *want*
to crawl into it, which is to say, like I do,
Rauschenberg feared promising
comfort he could not, in fact, provide.

[

3—HUG SOMEONE QUICKLY THEN MOVE ON TO
SOMEONE ELSE: CONTINUE THIS UNTIL NEXT CUE
(do this seriously, quickly, and smoothly).

6 – The Lovers .

When you step out on the metal porch behind
my apartment to smoke, I wonder what shape
          smoke takes over the yard or in the alley.

When I go out with you, just to be close,
there's something thick in it, more than
nicotine, a set of red wings, a presence.

By now the trees have been stripped
by winter—quelled model Sodoms in gray ash.
I've never heard snake speech—pomegranate

seeds on a holiday we were glad was clanless.
          We translate *between* into *together*
lying in my twin bed, millennial glow

of iPhones cooling mint walls, the soft running
          of feet along calves. I want to learn
how to give you your injections, measured hand

helping to balance the body with what dwells
          inside the body—soon hair, definition
in back muscles and arms. I mean to say

          I can't wait to continue together, naked,
having sex everywhere. We'll always be poor;
smoke, mountain, angel above it and all.

Fielding Dawson, a Black Mountain College student, tells of a scene in the summer of 1951. Rauschenberg and Cy Twombly, accompanied by Robert Motherwell, together create *Untitled (Night Blooming)*:

> Rauschenberg and Twombly on the gravel patio . . . gazing down at a large canvas, covered in most part by tar. . . . They tossed handfuls of pebbles on it. Motherwell, between them, gestured. Said to throw more on and they did. "More." And they did. "More." And they did.

[

Rauschenberg has such ease
with the everyday,

especially newspaper clippings—
gossip, the funnies, the nothings that hold
the world together.

In his later years he uses street signs,

photographs of his son Christopher,
paintings by or photos of his lovers, his (ex)wife,
the natural detritus of having lived—

a higher frequency, a rococo
timbre—not life as it could be, but is, just now.

Canyon (1969)

oil,
graphite, paper,
photograph
of artist's son,
            manufacturer's
tag, postcard,
printed reproductions,
flattened industrial
metal canister, paint
tube, wooden knob,
cardboard box, and other materials
on canvas with oil
on taxidermied bald eagle,
wood beam, and pillow
suspended by fabric

[

Art as context exercise—
no making,
no original content,
only placement of one
next to another.

Artist as:
            fussiest framer,
            most careful magpie.

[

Once upon a time, *Rhyme* housed a goat. The goat traveled, over the course of a number of years, through three different compositions, but *Rhyme* was home—goat mounted to painting mounted to wall.

Are we all required to be shepherds?
What will I steal from myself? What will I tear from this body?
[

[ERASED CAROLYN FORCHÉ POEM]

[

You look into the eyes
of an animal, long dead,
and, even as they are
glass, you see a field
warped with color and light.

7 – The Chariot .

A poet refuses to drive her car anywhere.
She says she can't do things—call the bank,

make an appointment at the dentist, pay a bill—

though we all know she can. She's always whispering
with two sphinxes out behind her apartment—plush
paws, sharp tongues. Of course she's brilliant,

a constellation of decoupage stars cut from glossies
pasted on a box for her piece, *Glitterbaby*.

We talk about what it means to hate
our armor. We talk sometimes about shots
of whiskey. Then we stop talking and drink.

She's falling in love again, after leaving
the guy who snorted cocaine in Seattle.

She's from a desert, too, but is better at building
a new city on the riverbank. One day

getting in her car and driving some place

built of wet stone, she will enter the city.
She will read them her poems. Like I do,
they will love her, will ask her where she's been.

"The desert," she'll say. "Umbrella shade by a chlorine
pool." She will read another poem, the sphinxes
will dance queer backstage, headlights still on.

Factum I & *Factum II* (1957)

oil, ink, pencil,
crayon, paper, fabric, newspaper, printed
reproductions, and painted paper on canvas
[painted simultaneously, neither one of these
paintings is an imitation of the other] *[[I wanted*
to explore] the role that accident played in my work
. . . I wanted to see how different, and in what
way, would be two different paintings that looked
that much alike. Rauschenberg claimed he
couldn't see any difference between the two
paintings, which I saw for the first time
hanging side by side. The differences apparent,
though the rhyme was unmistakable—a
couplet's thrall.] Gay?

Factum I & II (1957)

oil. Paper, ink, pencil,
crayon paper, fabric, newspaper, printed
reproductions, and painted paper on canvas
[painted simultaneously, neither one of these
painting is an imitatio of the other] [*[I wanted
to ecplore] the role that accident played in my work
. . . I wanted to see how different, and in what
way, would be two differnt paintngs that looked that
much alike.* Ruashcenbery claimed he
couldn'y see any difference between the two
paintings, which I saw for the first time
hanging ide by side. The differences apparent,
though the rhyme was unmistakable—a
couple's thrall.] Gay.

[

7—MOVE CLOSER TOGETHER

8 – Strength .

You can understand it, right? Holding
a sharp bone so close to the throat?

I saw it as a good omen, jaws closed
gently, like a stubborn door, by some careful force

—petal curve of hands. No one asks the lion
why he wants to open his mouth, you know

what I mean? I mean they imagine it, the blood of it,
the squelch of a desire we all have, somewhere—

to give in to the wet inside us,
that large, smooth blood clot knock,

shaped so it moves other blood around it.
When it repeats it becomes a pair

of sanguine prophecies: the lion kills
the young girl; the young girl lives.

I thought, for a long time, I'd hold this close,
the hope of return, so I let the lion open

his mouth. He said something. I said nothing
back. He said something else. I said nothing back.

Leaving, he said "lion lion lion," which I think was meant
to frighten me, but fear lives in lunge and paw thump

and lights out. The word *lion* strengthens like pulsing,
perceptible, but vital only to the body that holds it in.

Immediately after winning the Golden Lion at the 1964 Venice Biennale for a series of silkscreen paintings, Rauschenberg calls a friend in New York and tells him to cut each screen from its frame and then to burn them all—an excision from the body of his work, like an inflamed appendix, the expectation that he would or could repeat himself—excision, too, like exorcism.

[

Lacuna—anatomically,
a cavity or depression—a term
used often to describe
the structural hollows in bones.

Lacuna's root is *pool*
or *lake* in Latin,
            an anatomy of water.

[

The status of *Erased de Kooning Drawing* as a piece of art hinges entirely, and ironically, on narrative. Because of the deep antinarrative of the content, the utter transparency of it, all of its draw is found in the story of its origin, which takes the shape of a kind of trust between de Kooning and Rauschenberg, who held de Kooning in very high, though not uncritical, esteem. The greater work in this relationship was obviously on the part of de Kooning, who gave Rauschenberg something to erase only because he understood Rauschenberg's aim and refused to stifle the creative impulse of another artist; de Kooning allowed Rauschenberg to unmake/remake the piece so that, in its de Kooningian form, it ceased to exist. Rauschenberg's blank shout becomes de Kooning's small swath of permanent, voluntary silence. The piece is unexpectedly emotive because of this mingling—surprising subtlety, deep conversation, oral history, legend for a map made only of lakes.

[

Layers of white lead paint.
White is not blank, nor is it pure.

[

The corners of the undrawing have smudges now,
where he held it down, the inevitable
                                        residue of erasure.

[

[ERASED ROBERT HASS POEM]

[

Erase traced back:
to scrape or *to scrape*
    out—

white always, then, a symbol of violence.

[

In the handwritten request that his *White Paintings* be repainted, Rauschenberg had Billy (his friend? assistant? lover?) write:

> They are not [red box drawn around "not"] to be labeled
> as copies or reproductions but simply dated
> 1951 ["dated" and the year with shared underline
> in the same red as the box around "not"].

9 – The Hermit .

The moving makes one wise, dearest.
She's in Berlin now—the holidays—with her cat
 and a man. I knew her by her loss

of a different man, the poems she wrote about that.
 We met at a party in a dark, old house—
ornate, green wallpaper—later drinking red together,

buying glasses when a bottle would have been
wetter longer for less. She read all the words in the river,
 like an engineer rerouted it, made the bank

inhabitable—another piece breaks from the slab
 of absence at the center of the universe. She was first
to put a star in the lantern, wanting to know why

there's only one word like *scar* for the spirit—*injury*
sewn into *healed*. She said to be patient
 with myself, said it is possible to find the thing

one's supposed to do. Grabbing the star handle,
 she swung it over the streets rough with slush
and the blue salt of the city. And what of Ohio?

Cincinnati, its German food, its seekers
like students you'll find anywhere—clueless,
 eager to make lanterns of their own, with help.

Monogram (1955–1956)

oil, paper, fabric,
printed paper, metal,
wood, rubber shoe
heel, and tennis ball
on two conjoined
canvases with oil
on taxidermied
Angora goat with brass
plaque and rubber
tire on wood platform
mounted on four casters

[

Rauschenberg bought the goat, already taxidermied, at an office furniture store for a down payment of fifteen dollars on his assurance to the shopkeeper that he'd bring another fifteen dollars later. After two months, Rauschenberg returned to find the store shuttered—later he joked in an interview that he feared the shopkeeper would see *Monogram* in a magazine, recognize the goat, and request the rest of his money.

10 – Wheel of Fortune .

There were four flat clouds in the sky today—
I counted. I think I have too many books

and am haunted by images of collapsing
through the ceiling of the apartment below—

underness of disaster. I ascended the stairs
this morning, having forgotten my keys again,

and wondered if I'd dodged something, a car,
a brandished knife. There was a night

last week when a cat with green eyes
followed me home. He grew, paws large

as hands. His tag literally read, *Trouble.*

Warm already, it's raining in December, grass
persistently visible, ground wet and holding

itself against everything. I don't even need the heat
clicking in the radiator at the end of the bed.

But the landlord controls everything, and the water
filter on the kitchen faucet fell off again.

Last night for half an hour I tried
reattaching it—the circle of the faucet's mouth

stripped of its teeth.
The hallway smells of unlit gas.

My family traces an artery back to two hearts:

we are descendants

of John Blair, first Supreme
Court chief justice and signer of the Constitution,

and of my great-grandfather, Bon, whom I knew
well enough to see how little
he liked his faggy great-grandchild.

Bon, a bomber pilot, said he
bombed a barracks only
hours after Hitler was there.

Blood clot in the artery:

I learned from census records
my family enslaved at least three people
in Tennessee during the Civil War.

When I mention it to the family, it is called *a shame*,
called *the slavery element*. Someone says,

I suspect everyone might find some slavery
in their background. . . . It wasn't just
an American thing.

I'm reminded my grandmother says
(mother tongue of whiteness
being idiocy and empire)

she's one-sixteenth Cherokee.

I say I have to go, only to stare
at the ceiling for an unspecified amount of time.

[

8—MOVE APART

11 – Justice .

If we think of it as a door, the room it opens
        into is a walk-in closet with dresses and suits.
There are ways of cutting things out: a small knife,
        a surgery behind a curtain, then the heal.
One imagines balance as a kind of inaction,
        getting things to settle and leaving them. And it is,
for a while—my mother asks about my boyfriend,
        but I don't tell her about my floral dresses.
For Halloween I went as an icon, panty hose
        already with a run in it, tip of bowler, bustier,

and the highest heels I've ever seen. Turning

        my ankle I couldn't walk, even barefoot afterward.
Cause: queerness. Effect: a subtle rippling
        then a stillness. I would wipe the slate clean,
but the slate is a cheese grater—I would clean the slate
        like the whiteboard in class: *your assignment*
is to be everything. Simple enough really, expectation
        being only the act of doing the thing one does.
I think we will know how much a word weighs
        someday, science being what it is—feather
to the heart's red brick, quiet pillars, scale.

12 – The Hanged Man .

There's difficulty in the liminal glow,
serene strain of being tied upside down

to a living bow—leaves, no flowers yet.

Today I wear the blue dress, yellow
slippers—my hem resists gravity, clings to thighs,
red tights. All the blood in my head like light

leaks out in the shape of a thrift-store plate,
chipped on the rim even before I get it home.

I think of gymnasts, the year I spent
hardening my body—I was nine and already
our coach's shorts were apocalyptic, his thighs,

their thick tone. I quit before he taught me how
to spring back on my hands, but I can still stick
a round-off. Landing hurts my shins—*force*

meant to translate to *wider motion*. I imagine
him, Gabe, how young he must've been,

how in my mind he's suspended there—twenty-
three, twenty-four, my age now. How unlike me he was,

probably still is—an iron cross, face flushed,

arms all twitch and clench. He'd dismount heels over
head, land. We'd both breathe out together.

Listening to an interview with Rauschenberg
when he was in his seventies—his slow oil
country drawl, the playful turn of his mouth
—he reminds me, spectrally, of Bon.

[

When we look inside the dead goat,
there are still bones in its legs, its skull
and torso as simple as smudges,
smooth and liver-like in the X-ray.

The wool still falls like water. Wires and rods
hold everything in place and the tire is, yes,
tire—Rauschenberg must have scavenged it
from some alley—riddled with nails, in short, a flat.

The head, a violence of nails where horns meet
new and perfect skull, is cobbled invisibly—
            like a shoe, like a history.

[

I erased it, but I'll share what Ashbery said, "I cannot explain the action of leveling."

[

White is not blank, nor is it pure.

13 – Death .

The sun sets so early this far north, four,

//

half past. I've never seen a ship in the water.

//

In Duluth, I saw a freighter midair, suspended

//

in the shipyard, gray, angular weight. Superior

//

froze over that year and all of us, friends

//

then, drove from Minneapolis to see the cave

//

teeth, or ice formations, along the coast.

//

Once there, we walked a different route across

//

the wider part of the gulf instead of with everyone else

//

along the shore where the snow was pressed into ice;

//

later The Empress would crack her head slipping on it.

//

She'd be fine, but the whole time I'd been thinking

//

about the waist-thick stalactites, just hanging

//

from the red rocks—how easy an accident.

//

We all had on our black coats, rasping sweaters,

//

two pairs of wool socks, and boots, wool-lined.

//

We carried no flags—no true discovery

//

to be made. But when was there? Children pointing

//

at the tips of icicles, crawling beneath ice domes.

//

We found a keyholed alcove with two towers,

//

the sun between, something kicking against the clouds
        from within the clouds.

Oracle (1962–1965)

five-part found-metal
assemblage with five concealed
remote-controlled radios:
exhaust pipe on metal axle
and pushcart wheels; automobile
door on wheeled typewriter
table, with crushed metal; ventilation
duct, water, and concealed
showerhead in washtub on wheels,
with chain, wire basket, and metal
lid on wheels; constructed
            staircase control
unit housing automobile
tire and batteries
and other electronic components on wheels;
and wooden window frame
with ventilation duct
on wood support with wheels,
dimensions variable

[

In short, a careful car wreck—
            a loud and mobile home.

14 – Temperance .

Three blocks from my apartment there's a bar
			that used to be a real dive.
Now its lights are too bright for that to be true.
			I go there when there's nothing
else to do—a neon-sharp beer, something fried.

My favorite waiter, Cooper, brings their pitcher,
			refills my small cup with water;
they don't do this for anyone else. They live where I do,
			between two cardinal directions.

Their hair is longer than they'd like, they say,
			black boot sitting in a small pool
of beer someone spilled before I got here, bleeding
			into the industrial carpet. A pyramid,
Eye of Providence crossed out in black sharpie,

on their shirt, a blonde sun bursting through
			the dome of their flipped cap. Out back
past the pool tables, up a single step people smoke
			and hassle the cute ones.

Cooper knows how to handle the drunks, the grabs,
			the "ma'ams." Smiling, they lift their hand
in a blunt sign; two irises stitched into their arm.

Rauschenberg meets Susan Weil in Paris
where they both study at the Académie Julian.

They marry at the Weil family home
in Connecticut in 1950; a year later

Christopher is born. A year later
they are separated. A year later divorced.

[

6—WOMEN BRUSH HAIR

[

There is a photo of Rauschenberg and Weil young and in Paris in 1948. Rauschenberg carefully cuts Weil's hair in the doorway of the boarding house in which they lived on rue Stanislas. Weil holds something in her hands on her lap, likely her fresh-shorn hair.

The photo remains in Weil's personal collection.

[

Weil says, "I couldn't stay married to Bob.
But in my whole life I never had a fight with him.
I never had a cross word with him.
I loved him right up until he died."

[

1951: Weil visits Black Mountain College where Rauschenberg and Twombly have been spending the summer in the midst of an affair. Soon after arriving, Weil leaves with their newborn son, whom she brought with her. Weil divorces Rauschenberg, and he returns to Black Mountain in the winter of the following year.

[

As everyone played music in the Black Mountain dining hall,
Rauschenberg quite unremarkably stood and left. He walked
directly

and quite a ways out
into the January water
of a lake nearby
called Eden.

In the middle of the water—surrounded on all sides by trees and the makings of many of Rauschenberg's early experiments—ready to die, he moaned, his voice catching against—what? It remains impossible to say:

That he was gay; that this project,
like so many others already, had failed.

[

Rauschenberg, from the German
for *mountain* and *the moaning*

made by the wind through trees
or over a body of water.

15 – The Devil .

I read parts of Heidegger's *Being and Time* in undergrad.
Parts of those parts stuck with me, mostly
the inevitability of failure (like trying to read Heidegger).
We set out to be all things and never get there.
It's built in. Didn't seem like much then,
but it's untangled some section of the knot
at the center of things. The chain lengthened,
thickening my orbit around the altar on which a figure
hunches, looking at me, delicate wings, warm paws,
the queer dark inked in around their shoulders.
They're not evil, neither misshapen nor broken.
They are the puzzle piece I ate at five.
Others are also in the dark; when we look at the figure
beneath the upturned star, we see our own faces
not grimacing, not sad, not even bad likenesses,
just us, there, disappointed, tired, ready to watch Netflix
for six hours straight, to stay in the house for two days.
I order in another sandwich because I should eat
even if I won't be hungry. Craig delivers this time—
at least he comes to the door. He bends his head,
red cap hiding his face, to ignore my hair, its horns.

Untitled (1954)

oil, newspaper,
          fabric, printed
reproductions, and train
ticket made out to Edwin
P. Twombly Jr. (Cy Twombly),
on stretched umbrella
          fabric with wood
frame, light bulb, and electric cord

[

Like looking at a lake, no?
Heavy flatness, origin's blank
violence beneath
          skin, held within it:

lake—some celestial impact, maybe;
paper—a moonsworth of emptying.

[

5—TAKE OUT A HANDKERCHIEF AND WIPE YOUR OWN NOSE (do not blow).

[

Automobile Tire Print
(1953)

tire-tread mark (front
wheel) and tire-tread
          mark with house

paint (back wheel)
made by John
Cage's Ford Model A
driven by Cage over twenty sheets
of typewriter paper fastened
            together with library
paste, mounted on fabric

[

Rauschenberg and Cage
were, for a number of years,

romantically involved—
was it

the result of how
they were everywhere

inside one other's heads,
so everywhere inside one

another's work, so everywhere
inside one another?

[

Rauschenberg takes a photograph of Cage
in the Model A in 1952.

The photograph is solid
and warm, pristine, a set
of portals in the black

means by which one gets from one
place to another, somewhere

anyone can live
like someone else
finally for the first time.

[

John was fascinated by the fact that we were doing this. And he did a good job.

[

Reading Dante's *Inferno* to prepare for a series of prints, Rauschenberg becomes angry with Dante for being such a product of his time as he learns the punishment for sodomites: walking forever across hot sands.

In the print for this canto, Rauschenberg includes his own footprint in red ink.

[

Cage and Rauschenberg fall out in 1967 over professional differences, philosophic or romantic it's difficult to say, since both were so closely mingled in the lives of each artist. Their silence lasts ten years, broken when they reunite on the occasion of collaborating on *Travelogue* with Merce Cunningham (a past lover to both men).

[

Handwritten time score for the projector operator
from John Cage for *Theater Piece No 1*,
staged at Black Mountain in 1952—
the staging included four white paintings:

> Begin at 16 min
> play freely until 23 min
>
> Begin at 24:30
> play freely until 35:45
>
> Begin at 38:20
> play freely until 44:25

[

Jasper Johns and Rauschenberg meet in 1954 and become, as was Rauschenberg's usual habit, creative and romantic presences in one another's lives. This was two years after Rauschenberg's divorce from Weil, so also two years after he returns from Morocco and Italy with Cy Twombly, the divorce's catalyst, whose time with Rauschenberg would overlap and lead to the years spent with Johns, Cage, Cunningham, et al.

[

> 9—MEN TAKE OFF JACKETS;REPLACE THEM;REPEAT.

16 – The Tower .

Through the north window of the café, across
the parking lot of the laundromat, there's a building,
four stories, stripped of siding, windows wrapped in plastic.

A banner says, "European-style luxury apartments,"

freeing itself from the side of the building. The disaster
of investing in the best possible outcome, in believing

one can build anything. Electrified like cash in the hand,
the sight of naked studs, the pink paint sprayed in a schematic
          of power, or water, maybe, over the bones.

I'd feel bad but I don't—if you have enough money
to sell "European" to grad students, you have enough
to be stupid, but safe; I condemn most what I recognize

in myself, the meager structure, the standing in the midst.

I am neither built nor being built. And the suddenness
of it, of finding yourself unfinished—a quiet, steady dread.

You'd always known the roof would cave in on you.
You knew there was something yellow in your pale
bones waiting to catch fire. Question: is the dull sheen

of plastic a cocoon or evidence of things mummified—
          can encasement be both? Someday
someone will set fire to it and, burning, it will be a light.

Short Circuit (1955)

oil, fabric, notebook
paper, postcard, printed
reproductions of Abraham
Lincoln and of Lorenzo
di Credi's painting *Venus* (c. 1493),
autograph of Judy Garland,
and program from
an early John Cage
concert, given with David
Tudor, on canvas,
wood supports, and cabinet
            with two hinged
            doors containing
a painting by Susan Weil
            and "an Original
Sturtevant" captioned
by Rauschenberg and created
by Elaine Sturtevant
            in 1967 to replace
            a Jasper Johns flag
painting that had originally
been included but was stolen in 1965

[

Poetry as imperialist project:
to see, claim, repurpose,
gather, frame,

remove from cradle, erase.

[

Deep in our line
my family is related
to a man beheaded

by Queen Elizabeth I
for attempting
to marry Mary,

Queen of Scots, thereby
allowing her to ascend
to the English throne.

He was the son
of the first English poet
to write, supposedly,

in the sonnet
form, the first
cousin of Anne Boleyn.

They too died
by beheading.
Each of the three

was important
and, so, painted

with their heads
still attached.

[

To erase—to depict an animal
head or limb with a jagged edge
as if it had been ripped
from the body—as in a coat
                                        of family arms.

[

When I think of scraping out
I see arm elbow-deep in a white stag,

arrow still in heart and hunt
just ended. Practical scoop

of gut and color
onto the ground. It's amazing

how grotesque the workings are that keep
things going, how swollen with blood.

You have to erase heart,
lungs, spleen, and liver,

the glut of intestine, the bladder,
to make use of what's left. Sure, something ends

for you—some of the dogs
are still barking—but this body

can do more than keep itself going.

17 – The Star .

Without even trying, after seven years, regeneration,
 the whole thing, the unending pour of the body
into the world with its own blue bodies, its hardness. Lucky,

isn't it? Not even the stars earn a new body, arms
 reaching out and snapping. They do die, though,
twice—once in the dark and once in the dark

of the eye. This is old like birdsong—
 rising swirl, steep drop. Or gray squirrels
diving from the rooftop of the unused garage

into the leaf-empty tree by the garden.
 So much yellow paint—the buildings,
the black velvet dress hung in the closet God hides in.

They're genderqueer. I'd say They grow
 Their hair out. I'd say They drape cloth.
I'd say that because I'd love God if They were.

I'd be closer to Their image and They'd be fabulous too.
 We'd go to the 19—$2.50 rum and cokes. "You don't need
a double, honey," the bartender would tell Them,

like he told my friend from out of town, a writer
 who strengthens his body with anxiety—
all we have is the body, its extend, bend, its spark and break.

To paint, take one
            or many
and flatten into one.

Rauschenberg takes everything
but lets each edge stay.

I want poems like this—
            all edge and gather and mine.

18 – The Moon .

What lives in the depths couldn't pick the moon out
of a lineup. What lives in the depths only knows what it feels

when the moon gently pulls from between towers at night,
reflecting a thing further away than anyone has ever been,

the anger in it, the wolf light, calmed, practical now, a hunting
dog, a hunter's red moon on the river. Rent in two,

the earth and its satellite—dirt rib, celestial Eve, vigilant
Diana tracing the shape of her bow across the dark,

and the man, too, lounging in gray craters, his pale
eyelids, his feminine curve. The moon: a symbol for nothing

except maybe what it's like to understand you can see
only one side of something. Even so, grass is green and wet

with rain, a thousand convex portraits of the world, a thousand
apocalypses. There's a trail out over the sea,

one the eye follows. On the waves a stone disk cobbled
from light, its starkness warbling, an organismic bend.

It's night, or it isn't. The moon is there or it is there
and you can't see it. I've missed every eclipse since

I knew to look for them—interruption of dying
star, silent passing-over—and I want so much to see

the true face of the moon, its sadness, its genuine dark.

When I was young,
Abraham and Isaac were,
somehow, white:

Now no angel,
no ram—the blade must meet
Isaac's throat, must cut white.

[

[ERASED GEORGE W. BUSH PAINTING] [ERASED CONSTITUTIONAL FRACTION] [ERASED KENNY GOLDSMITH PERFORMANCE ON YOUTUBE] [ERASED WILLIAMS POEM] [ERASED WHITMAN POEM] [ERASED QUOTE FROM *GONE WITH THE WIND*; FROM MARGARET SANGER; FROM HARVEY MILK; FROM MILEY CYRUS; FROM BOBBY KENNEDY] [ERASED DREADS ON A WHITE MAN ON THE A TRAIN] [ERASED POLICE TRAINING SEMINAR VIDEO] [ERASED ABRAHAM LINCOLN SPEECH] [ERASED WELL-MEANING FACEBOOK POST FROM "COLORBLIND" AUNT] [ERASED SUPREME COURT DECISION] [ERASED LOGBOOK OF CITIZENS SENT TO JAPANESE INTERNMENT CAMPS] [ERASED NFL TEAM MASCOT] [ERASED TONY HOAGLAND POEM] [ERASED MAP OF COLFAX, LOUISIANA, 1873] [ERASED MAP OF THE UNDERGROUND RAILROAD] [ERASED QUOTE FROM MY GREAT-GRANDFATHER] [ERASED MINNEAPOLIS POLICE DEPARTMENT STATEMENT ON THE DEATHS OF PHILANDO CASTILE AND JUSTINE DAMOND] [ERASED PASSAGES FROM ENSLAVERS' WILLS FREEING THE ENSLAVED AFTER THEIR DEATHS] [ERASED SUSAN B. ANTHONY COIN] [ERASED CHRISTINE JORGENSEN PAPARAZZI SHOT] [ERASED YA BASKETBALL NOVEL FEATURING PROTAGONIST OF COLOR WHO JUST WANTS TO BE "NORMAL"

WRITTEN BY WHITE AUTHOR (#615 OF INFINITE)] [ERASED COLUMBUS CARGO LOG] [ERASED PHOTO OF WHITE HANDS HOLDING BLACK HANDS IN BIRMINGHAM] [ERASED RED HAT WITH WHITE TEXT]

[

So many layers of white lead paint
it was too heavy and had to be abandoned.

White is not blank, nor is it pure.

19 – The Sun .

I didn't know I needed this until I needed it
more than anything—think soft, pink skull,
red jolt of fabric, wind-swollen, a horse the following shade:
[   ]

There are no east-facing windows here, just the wall.

I try to feel duality manifest—
particle and wave defying their most basic definitions
simply by acting like one another.

So often I think on melanomas, the daily danger

of skipping sunscreen. Yet here I am again,
walking naked along my neighbors' retaining wall,
stacked stone, empty dirt stripped clean

to plant new foundations. By May I'll stop

being a student of certain things, become a better
student of others—trees are so like columns.
I can tell you melancholy melts like ice,

and that knowledge is a power plant. If we are a line,

I don't want to be at the front. I hate parades.
Even the gay ones go on too long. And children can stop
having children to have children—because, you know,

the sun will die after we do, but the sunflowers, those die with us.

Charlene (1954)

oil, charcoal,
printed reproductions,
newspaper, wood,
plastic mirror, men
's undershirt, umbrella,
lace, ribbons and other
fabrics, and metal
on Homasote, mounted
on wood, with electric light

[

Tenderness? Warmth?

[

> [2]—TOUCH TWO PLACES ON YOUR BODY WHERE YOU ARE TICKLISH (don't laugh)

[

Rauschenberg drank; I drink.
I can say little else about this now.

20 – Judgement .

It had been years since I picked up a trumpet—
imbalance of bell like a flower, sexual organs
now mechanisms, valves, and slides. It was only a matter

of time before I realized how bad I sounded, lips
numb and thick like bars of soap. Angelface played along
on the upright bass, another friend on the untuned
piano. Had everyone had more whiskey, it might have passed

as *experimental*, as something more than the end
of a world in which I knew how to play music.
But we played, and still, I felt that warm stir
in the long bones, the grammatical lean of noise.

We had exhumed the dead, their gray-hued children.
A friend has started dating another friend
after they spent a week together in Germany.
We are, the rest of us, glad to see it, the closing

of a large loop, a collapsing of one thing into another.
A caldera, blue of lake sunk in volcanic middle like a stone,
that utter transformation from fire so hot the earth gives
up the ghost, to such a wet stillness that the mountain

simply repeats the word *sky*, the clouds passing over
that open mouth—not quite a bell but a sounding.

Rauschenberg decides to place the taxidermied
Angora goat in the middle
of the large square platform of *Monogram.*

I see the goat for the first time in his plastic
cube, preserved like a bog
mummy in the unflattering light of the museum.

I look very closely at him—I want to touch his eye
—blink, little guy, pull away.

[

In his later years, Rauschenberg traveled the world as an activist and took photographs (a medium his son would later work in). In a journal from that time:

My preoccupation with photography in the beginning (1949) was first supported by a personal conflict between shyness and curiosity. The camera functioned as a social shield.

In 1981 I think of the camera as my permission to walk into every shadow or watch while any light changes. Mine is the need to be where it will always never be the same again; a kind of archaeology in time only. Forcing one to see whatever the light or the darkness touches, and care. My concern is to move at a speed within which to act.

[

I wonder if Rauschenberg ever dreamt
of the original de Kooning drawing,
if he could still see it

even in those last days, behind the surface
scratching its way out, smelling of rubber
and ink and gold leaf,
sitting there, just behind,
like some amoebic worm in the eye—
unrelenting, athrash.

Untitled (Man with White Shoes) (1954)

oil, pencil, crayon, paper,
fabric, newspaper clippings (including
an article and photographs
related to the twenty-fifth wedding
anniversary of Rauschenberg's parents
and another related
            to his sister Janet's coronation
in a local beauty pageant),
photograph of artist's sister Janet,
his son Christopher, and Jasper Johns,
a handwritten letter
from Christopher, and drawings
by Jack Tworkov and Cy
Twombly, all on wood and canvas,
including an earlier *Black Painting*
by the artist (c. 1951), with glass,
mirror, tin, cork,
a pair of the artist's socks
and painted leather shoes, dried
grass, and taxidermied Plymouth Rock
hen, on wood structure
mounted on five casters

[

            As I stand in front
of *Erased de Kooning Drawing* again, I see myself
in the glass, head like a bruise-
hued fish scale fallen, holy now, from an eye.

It's not really blank, is it?
Some smudges knit
still into the paper's structure?

21 – The World .

I have at least four selves: first self, star-crossed bull,
second self, disembodied human head in profile

(the body tried so little to understand the head,
the head left the body behind), third self, winged,

fourth self, toothed. These selves bleed into
the bowl of my body. Some days I am

a birdtooth, some a minotaur, a mermaid,
a smear, a cut, a heartworm. Some days I lie

in the exact center of the bed and count heartbeats
like calendar squares. I see myself in other people

and I want to fuck them, hoping to close
the distance between this self (myself) and the self

(myself) that looks like them. The best day will be the day
I fold myself into Hermes, tie pronouns to my shoes like wings.

If I am made from the clay of the earth, someone throw me
into a new shape every day, someone break me every night.

When people ask me what I want, I say nothing,
not because I don't know, but because I don't know if what I want

includes them knowing that I want to be a beautifulnothing
            —beautifulnothing hips, beautifulnothing tits,
a beautifulnothing dick—backlit, an ecstatic shadow ruin.

Rauschenberg would later reveal
                    the presence of a second
unerased drawing behind his undrawing.

[

With the exception of the singing (cue 10), this should be a QUIET *piece.* X *will give you your cue to stand and look at the audience. When this cue is given, turn toward the audience and stand still without any show of recognition. After* X *cue is shown, it will take 10 seconds for the lights to come on fully. While the lights are on,* REMAIN FIXED *until the lights die down and go completely out. When the lights are* COMPLETELY OUT, *exit through the same door you entered.*

If you have coats and purses, wear them. Leave nothing downstairs. You should disappear as mysteriously as you appeared.

[

Rauschenberg dies quietly
          of heart failure
on a Monday in the new millennium
on Captiva Island in the Gulf

after a personal decision to turn
off the machines keeping him alive.

[

10—SING ONE OF THE 10 SONGS
BEING SUNG (LOUDLY), OR SING A SONG
OF YOUR OWN CHOICE.

[

To some, this performance might be easy—to others, difficult. In any case, it is real.

[

Rauschenberg on *Monogram*:

I finally decided to just leave him alone,
let him simply stand there elegantly in a field.

[

4—DRAW A RECTANGLE IN THE AIR AS
HIGH AS YOU CAN REACH.

Acknowledgments

Thanks especially to Diane Seuss for selecting *Major Arcana: Minneapolis* as the winner of the Burnside Review Chapbook Prize, and to Natalie Eilbert for selecting *White Combine: A Portrait of Robert Rauschenberg* for the *Atlas Review* chapbook series. These two chapbooks have been spun together to create this book, a third thing with its own unique beauty.

On page 17, Charles Olson's poem "These Days" is quoted in its entirety. Works by Charles Olson published during his lifetime are copyright the Estate of Charles Olson; previously unpublished works are copyright the University of Connecticut. "These Days" has been used with their permission.

Thanks to Saltonstall Foundation for the Arts, where I worked on an ancestrally related version of this manuscript, and especially to Lesley Williamson and Chef Mandy for making Ithaca the most perfect place on earth to spend a September.

Thanks to Vermont Studio Center, where I worked through a manuscript that, while textually not related to this work, was conceptually related to the idea of a single-poem book and makes an appearance as "the river" in "9 – The Hermit."

Thanks to Poets House for honoring me with an Emerging Poets fellowship, which allowed for the completion of this book. To Anselm Berrigan for his amazing and thoughtful engagement with this project, and to my other fellows, Rabih Ahmed, Kiran Bath, Catherine Chen, Charlene François, Shalewa Mackall, James Fujinami Moore, Val Rigodon, Sarah Sala, and Nicole Wallace.

Thanks to E. G. Asher for their generous feedback on this project in its earliest forms, and of course for their friendship, which I hold dearer than they might realize.

Thanks to Raena Shirali for her impossibly thorough reading of this book during a June week in the Adirondacks, and to my fellow workshop participants Laura Cresté, Jen DeGregorio, Tim Lynch, Ebs Sanders, and Evan Gill Smith.

Thanks to all of my writing teachers over the years for getting me to the point where I could write this: Luci Tapahonso, Natalie Scenters-Zapico, Lisa Chavez, Laurel Coffey-Bodine, Michael Thomas, Peter Campion, Ray Gonzalez, Trish Hampl, Charlie Baxter, Garrard Conley, Rebecca Lindenberg.

Thanks to all of my poetry siblings and community members for being so generous in so many ways: Anna Rasmussen, Mike Alberti, Alexandra Watson, Emily Strasser, Roy Guzman, Gabrielle Calvocoressi, Leila Chatti, Tiana Clark, Jake Skeets, Brian Teare, CAConrad, Peter LaBerge, Ron Mohring, Matt Rasmussen, Kenzie Allen, Chen Chen, Gretchen Marquette, T. C. Tolbert, Rick Barot, Tracy K. Smith, sam sax, Jane Huffman, Ander Monson, G. C. Waldrep, Jameson Fitzpatrick, Morgan Parker, and a long list of others I can't include here. Whether you knew it or not, by supporting my work through publication or simply kind words, you made it possible for me to keep writing, so I can't thank you enough.

Great thanks to my parents, Kelly and Brian Ketner, for encouraging my various false starts (gymnastics, painting, printmaking, music). Without everything I learned from those practices and from you, this book never could have come to be. Special thanks to my mother, a visual artist in her own right, for instilling in me a deep love and appreciation for the arts and most of all for introducing me to Rauschenberg's piece *Bed* at a formative age.

And my final and greatest thanks to Cormac, love of my life, for your indulgence, excellent cocktails, and endlessly reciprocated love.

Notes

The unattributed quotations in italics in this text are from Robert Rauschenberg.

This book is deeply informed by and in conversation with the Museum of Modern Art's 2017 *Robert Rauschenberg: Among Friends* retrospective and the accompanying exhibition monograph, which I bought after seeing the show five times. The following essays from the book were sources for the biographical, anecdotal, and critical information about Rauschenberg and his work and set off by high quality images of Rauschenberg's work; I also used them as references throughout the process of writing [*WHITE*]:

"Robert Rauschenberg: Five Propositions," by Achim Borchadt-Hume
"Disciplined by Albers: Foundations at Black Mountain College," by Leah Dickerman
"Made Out of the Real: Lessons from the Fulton Street Studio," by Hal Foster
"Disparate Visual Facts: Early Combines," by Branden W. Joseph
"Inevitable Fusing of Specializations: Experiments in Art and Technology," by Michell Kuo
"Gifts from the Street: Early Media Works," by Pamela M. Lee
"Pedestrian Color: The Red Paintings," by Helen Molesworth
"An Invitation, Not a Command: Silk-screen Paintings," by Richard Meyer

"Miniature Monument: Travel and Work in Italy and North Africa," by Kate Nesin

"Force of Contact: Objects and Performance," by Catherine Wood

The lists of materials that appear beneath a given title and year are repurposed directly from the monograph and the MoMA didactics that accompanied the pieces in their space. The line breaks are my own.

The Fielding Dawson quote on page 20 comes from *The Black Mountain Book.*

The numbered sections are reproduced verbatim from a letter to the cast of *Open Score* in the collection of the Getty Research Institute, except for the section marked with "[2]," where there is a typing error in the original that makes the assumed "2" illegible.

The anecdote about only paying for half of the taxidermied goat in "*Monogram*" comes from a 1998 television interview between Rauschenberg and Charlie Rose, in which the two walk together up the spiraling ramp of the Guggenheim Museum.

While writing the major arcana poems included here, I kept near me, as a reference, a full Rider-Waite-Smith deck, the most influential tarot deck in the western tradition, first compiled and illustrated in 1909.

www.ingramcontent.com/pod-product-compliance
Lightning Source LLC
LaVergne TN
LVHW051017080826
845145LV00009B/2663